Party
Fun
& Favors
in One!

CANDY
Creations

Sweet Treats to Build & Eat!

SHERIDAN COUNTY LIBRARY
100 West Laurel Ave.
Plentywood, MT 59254
406-765-2317

D0047351

Let's Get Started

Gather the supplies listed for each project you're making, and if working with younger children, do some prep work to simplify their decorating tasks. Set up a clean flat work area with plenty of space for each child. Then turn the kids loose to create their own party favors. Their cute creations may – or may not – make it home before the nibbling begins!

Reminders

- Wash and dry hands well before (and during) decorating.
- It's OK if kids' creations don't look exactly like the photos – the fun is in the decorating process!
- Plan for some messiness and offer kids aprons or old shirts to wear over their clothing.
- Let kids help with the clean-up.

Copyright © 2012 CQ Products
Waverly, IA 50677
All rights reserved.
No part of this book may be reproduced or transmitted in any form or by any means, electronic or mechanical, including photocopying, recording or by any information storage and retrieval system, without permission in writing from the publisher.

Printed in China

Distributed By:

507 Industrial Street
Waverly, IA 50677
$10.01 2/14
ISBN-13: 978-1-56383-421-9
ISBN-10: 1-56383-421-9
Item #2907

Helpful Do-Ahead Suggestions

1. Pre-cut small pieces and place in bowls for children to use.
2. Pre-cut or pre-assemble base pieces as needed so they are ready to decorate.
3. Sort candies and gather what each child needs on a paper plate.
4. Have damp washcloths or wipes available to clean off hands during decorating.
5. Unwrap candies just before use.

Helpful Tools to Use

Toothpicks: to apply small amounts of melted bark to candies or to move small candies

Tweezers: to pick up small candies and set them in place

Kitchen shears: to cut soft candies easily without mashing them

Waxed or parchment paper: to keep melted candy from sticking to the work surface

Table knife or back of spoon: to spread mixtures smoothly

Small plastic bags: to pipe on small amounts or lines of frosting, icing or melted mixtures (Simply spoon mixture into a bag, snip off a small corner and squeeze bag to pipe mixture out of hole.)

Adults should handle these jobs:

1. Melting almond bark or candy wafers in the microwave
2. Cutting with sharp knives (Tip: Warm up knife in hot water to make clean cuts in chocolate.)
3. Curling paper ribbon with edge of scissors
4. Using kitchen shears to cut firm chewy candies like jelly beans, licorice twists and Tootsie Rolls
5. Preparing plastic bags for piping icing or melted bark

Push Pop Planes

 for each

You'll Need

Prepare for take-off!
Blue skies ahead.

- 1 Push Pop candy
- 1 stick of gum in foil wrapper
- 1 rubber band
- 2 Life Savers
- 1 Airhead mini
- Melted almond bark
- 1 plain M&M

 optional   decorative paper, 3 x 4" mailing labels, stickers, markers, rubber stamps, clear tape, glue dots, etc.

To Make

1 Carefully lift "clip" of Push Pop and center gum under clip; release clip to hold gum in place.

2 Thread rubber band through hole of both Life Savers, centering Life Savers on rubber band. With Life Saver "tires" under Push Pop, bring one end of rubber band over one end of gum, hooking rubber band behind clip and crossing the front of Push Pop. Bring opposite end of rubber band over other end of gum, hooking behind clip and crossing front of Push Pop.

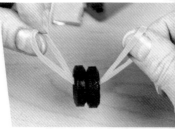

3 Cut a ⅜ x 2¼″ piece from Airhead to create a "propeller," cutting each end to a point. Slide propeller under crossed bands on front of Push Pop "plane" and center it behind bands. Using melted bark, attach M&M to the center of propeller.

try this

Replace Push Pop wrapper and paper gum wrapper (leaving foil wrapper in place) with decorative paper. Attach with glue stick. (See photo page 4.)

Candied Cooties

You'll Need

Creepy crawly cuties to make and devour!

- 1 Saf-T-Pop sucker, unwrapped
- 1 chocolate Swiss Roll or Ho-Ho
- Melted white or chocolate almond bark
- Assorted candies: Sour Punch Straws, Pull-n-Peel licorice (purple or red), Jelly Bellies, Smarties, mini M&Ms, writing icing (any color), Chewy Sweet Tarts Minis

To Make

1 To make antennae, cut 1˝ from looped end of sucker handle to leave two separate pieces still attached to sucker. Attach flat side of sucker to one end of Swiss Roll with melted bark, antennae up, for "face"; let dry.

2 Attach "legs" to Swiss Roll in one of these ways and let dry on waxed paper…

For long legs, cut six (3˝) strips of Sour Punch Straws or licorice. Attach strips to bottom of Swiss Roll with melted bark, legs extending out evenly from each side of "body." Cut Jelly Bellies in half and press cut side to end of each leg (or fasten with melted bark).

For short legs, set Swiss Roll on waxed paper and attach four Chewy Sweet Tarts along each side with melted bark.

3 For "eyes," attach a mini M&M to the center of a Smartie with melted bark. When set, attach eyes and a red mini M&M "mouth" to face with melted bark.

4 Draw squiggly lines of writing icing down length of Swiss Roll. Randomly attach M&Ms to icing while wet; let dry completely.

try this

Use candy necklace pieces for eyes and mouth. Insert a short thin piece of red Rips candy into mouth to make a long "tongue."

Watch This!

You'll Need

Edible food markers
1 giant Chewy Sweet Tart
1 tsp. light corn syrup
1 tsp. powdered sugar
Food-safe paintbrush
Candy decorating sprinkles
Bubble gum tape
1 stick of gum in foil wrapper
Melted white almond bark
Clear tape

Time for a sweet snack!

To Make

1 Use food markers to draw "hands" and/or numerals on Sweet Tart "watch." Mix corn syrup and powdered sugar. Brush a thin layer of mixture over watch "face" and add candy sprinkles to complete numerals and watch hands as desired; let dry at least 1 hour.

2 Cut a piece of gum tape about 8″ long (or to fit 1½ times around wrist). Cut one end into a point to make the watch "band." Use a toothpick to make a line of three or four small holes through band near pointed end, about ½″ apart.

3 To make a "buckle," tape foil wrapper closed down entire length of gum. Use melted bark to fasten straight end of gum tape across one end of foil wrapper on taped side, with edges even; let dry. Fold foil-wrapped gum around gum tape, overlapping on back side to finish buckle; tape in place. Bend buckle open slightly to create an opening for band.

4 Attach watch face to center of band with melted bark; let dry. To wear, wrap band around wrist and gently slide pointed end through buckle opening.

Tick Tock
Tick Tock

Zany Zebras

You'll Need

Stripes can drive a zebra crazy!

1″ piece of black licorice twist

Large gumdrops (1 white, 1 black)

1 Nutter Butter cookie

Melted white almond bark

1 small chocolate-covered mint patty, cut in half

2 pink Smarties

2 white York Pieces

Red writing icing

1 tube black decorating icing with a small round tip

To Make

1 With shears, cut licorice into skinny strips for zebra's "mane." Cut two narrow slices from each gumdrop; press sticky sides of a white and black slice together for each "ear." Set all pieces aside.

2 Dip cookie in melted bark to coat all sides; let excess bark drip back into bowl and set cookie on waxed paper. While bark is still wet, set mint patty half at one end of cookie for zebra's "snout," round edges even. Set Smarties on edge for "nostrils," along cut edge of mint patty. Arrange licorice strips near opposite end of cookie for mane; hold until set, about 1 minute.

3 Attach York Pieces below mane for "eyeballs."

4 With black icing, draw stripes on cookie as desired and add black "pupils" to eyeballs.

5 Attach set-aside gumdrop ears with melted bark.

6 Draw a "mouth" with red icing; let dry.

Li'l Licorice Baskets

for each

You'll Need

- 5 colored licorice twists (same color)
- ½ Salted Nut Roll
- Melted candy wafers (to match licorice)
- Plastic piping bag
- Dots candies
- Mini M&Ms

Tisket-a-Tasket, little flowers in a basket!

To Make

1 Slice off rounded end of candy bar half so chunk is flat on both ends; then cut chunk in half crosswise again.

2 To create "basket" base, stand both candy chunks upright on cut ends. Fasten flattest sides of chunks together using melted wafers; press together and hold until set.

3 Wrap one licorice twist around base to measure length; cut off excess. Cut three more licorice twists to correct length. Starting at the bottom, pipe melted wafers around base and attach one licorice twist; hold in place until set, about 2 minutes. Repeat with remaining trimmed licorice, lining up cut ends on back side of basket.

4 Cut the last licorice twist about 4½" long for "handle." Dip ends in melted wafers and press inside opposite edges of basket for handle; let dry.

5 To make each "flower," use shears to cut off rounded top of one Dot. Snip down partway through larger end of Dot three times to make six "petals." Gently separate petals and press one M&M into middle between cuts.

6 Cut green Dots into thin strips and arrange in basket like "grass." Fill basket with flowers.

try this

Fill basket with Easter egg candies.

Peep Mobiles

for each

You'll Need

This car says,
"PEEP PEEP!"

1 Twinkie, unwrapped

Melted white almond bark

4 pastel-colored Petite Mints

5 Life Savers (at least 4
of one color)

2 spice drop candies

Pull-n-Peel licorice, optional

1 Peeps bunny

14

To Make

1 Starting about 1″ from one end of Twinkie, cut and remove a piece from the top about 1¼″ long and 1″ deep.

2 Using melted bark, attach one Petite Mint "hubcap" to each of four same-colored Life Saver "tires," pointed side inside the hole. Let dry a minute, then attach completed "wheels" to the sides of Twinkie "car" with hubcaps facing out. Cut off ¼″ from rounded ends of two spice drops and attach cut side to front of car for "headlights."

3 Peel one individual string from licorice and cut to about 4″ in length for "seat belt." Wrap seat belt over one shoulder of bunny and diagonally across its midsection; attach both ends behind bunny using melted bark. Let dry, then set bunny in "driver's seat" cut-out.

4 Using melted bark, attach a Life Saver "steering wheel" to inside of cut-out, in front of Peep, with about half the steering wheel showing above car.

try this

Cut two thin round slices and a rectagular slice from additional spice drops and attach to back of car for "tail lights" and a "license plate."

15

Eye Candy

for each

You'll Need

Who's masquerading behind those eyes?

- 1 (1.55 oz.) Hershey's Milk Chocolate candy bar, unwrapped
- 1″ to 1¼″ round or half-round cookie cutter
- About 1⅓ yds. ribbon
- Clear tape
- Food-safe craft sticks*
- Melted white or chocolate almond bark (or colored candy wafers)
- 1 stick of gum, unwrapped
- About 25 York Pieces
- Nerds candies

To Make

1 Set candy bar flat side up on a flat, sturdy work surface. Using a sharp knife, carefully cut a mask shape from candy bar (draw a paper template as a pattern, marking eye location). Warm cookie cutter in hot water, dry and use to cut holes in candy bar for "eyes." (Use almond bark to repair any cracks in candy bar.) Flip chocolate mask over.

2 Cut ribbon into four 12″ lengths. Use tape to fasten end of one ribbon to one end of craft stick and wrap ribbon partway around stick. Hold remaining three ribbons against back side, near bottom of stick and continue wrapping the first ribbon around to the bottom of the stick to hold other ribbons in place; secure with tape.

3 Use melted bark to attach top of stick to center back of chocolate "mask." Add more melted bark over and around stick to secure it, if needed; let dry.

4 Cut gum in half crosswise. Use shears to cut several slits at cut end, about 1″ long. Use melted bark to attach to back of mask with "fringe" above eyes; let dry.

5 Carefully turn mask over so flat side is up. Cover about ¼ of flat side with melted bark. Immediately set York Pieces around edge in wet bark and sprinkle Nerds on remaining wet bark. Repeat with remainder of mask, ¼ at a time.

* Or cover stick with clingy plastic wrap.

17

The Write Candy

You'll Need

Finally – a pencil to chew on!

Colored paper

Decorative scissors

Double-stick tape

1 (1.7 oz.) roll Rolos

1 Hershey's Kiss in gold foil

1 stick of gum in foil wrapper

2 jumbo Smarties (same color)

Melted white almond bark

Black fine-tip marker

To Make

1 Cut colored paper into a rectangle, 3¾" x 4¾". Trim edge of one short side with decorative scissors for rippled look. Place strips of double-stick tape along all four edges of paper and another strip in the middle. Line up roll of Rolos on tape at one long edge and wrap paper tightly around candy to cover.

2 Expose tip of chocolate Kiss by peeling back a little foil ("pencil lead"). Cut off excess foil. With tape, attach flat side of Kiss to candy roll at rippled end of "pencil." (Kiss fits inside paper.)

3 For metal trim on pencil, unfold ends of gum's foil wrapper. Place a strip of tape along entire length of wrapper seam and wrap gum around other end of pencil, placing top edge even with paper.

4 Fasten Smarties together with melted bark to make "eraser"; let dry. With melted bark, fasten eraser to end of candy roll above metal trim. Let dry.

5 Use marker to print words such as "No. 2" or "Happy Birthday" on pencil.

Sweet Rides

 TRUCK

Fill this truck with a candy payload!

You'll Need

1 mini box Dots

Aluminum foil

Double-stick tape

10 Andes chocolates (red wrapper)

2 chocolate-coated Raspberry Sticks

4 red mini M&Ms

4 white Life Savers, unwrapped

2 yellow mini Chewy Sweet Tarts

Melted white almond bark

Waxed paper

Black permanent marker

To Make

1 Wrap Dots box in aluminum foil for "truck" base. Cover top of box with tape and press four Andes lengthwise onto tape, making truck's "hood" and "bed." The two back Andes should overhang box about ½".

2 Stack and tape three Andes across hood, halfway back, for truck's "cab." Wrap Raspberry Sticks in foil for "bumpers." Tape a bumper to front and back of box.

3 For sides of truck, tape one Andes lengthwise on opposite sides of truck bed. For "tailgate," attach one Andes on back end.

4 Using melted bark, attach one M&M to center of each Life Saver for "wheels." When dry, attach wheels to sides of truck base and Sweet Tarts ("headlights") to front of truck above bumper.

5 For "windshield," cut a half-circle from waxed paper and tape to front of truck cab. With marker, draw a "steering wheel" on windshield.

try this

Load the truck with chocolate candy rocks or Warheads Sour Chewy Cubes. Flip the tailgate down to unload.

for each TRACTOR

You'll Need
Items listed in **bold** on page 20, plus:

8 Andes mints (green wrapper)

Foil-wrapped chocolate coins (four 1½" and two 1")

1 yellow Life Saver, unwrapped

1 yellow Starburst

2 red mini M&Ms

1 mini Charleston Chew (or 1½" piece of black licorice twist)

To Make

1 Cover Dots box ("tractor" base) in foil as for truck. With tape, attach one Andes across one end of box and two Andes lengthwise on top of box for "hood." Tape two Andes upright on each side of exposed box to finish sides of tractor. Tape flat side of remaining Andes to uprights across back of tractor.

2 For "front wheels," tape a small coin to each side of box. To make each back wheel, tape two large coins together. With tractor on its side, tape a back wheel to upright candies, with bottom of wheel ½" below bottom of box. Turn tractor over and attach other wheel.

3 Using melted bark, attach Lifesaver "steering wheel" behind hood and Starburst "seat" between upright candies. Attach M&M "tail lights" to back uprights. To make "smokestack," wrap bottom ⅓ of Charleston Chew in foil. Twist and flatten end of foil to make a short tab. Slide tab between tractor hood candies.

Coral Critters

You'll Need

8 sour gummy worms
1 large gumdrop
1 Nerds Rope, unwrapped
Melted white almond bark

Taking a dip at the coral reef.

To Make

Cut off the desired colored section of each gummy worm for "tentacles." Arrange tentacles evenly around gumdrop "body," pressing cut ends against gumdrop to stick. Coil Nerds Rope and fasten end with melted bark; hold until set. Set octopus on top of coil, fastening in place with melted bark, if desired.

23

Sweet Dreams

You'll Need

There were four in the bed and the little one said... roll over!

2 Fruit Roll-Ups, any colors*

1 (1.5 oz.) Kit Kat candy bar, unwrapped

Parchment paper

White writing icing

4 Jordan almonds

4 Tootsie Fruit Rolls or Tootsie Roll Midgees, unwrapped

Edible food markers

To Make

1 To make "bed," cover at least half of one side of Kit Kat with one Fruit Roll-Up, pressing firmly over edges and to back side of candy bar to secure. Set on parchment paper.

2 Use writing icing to attach Jordan almond "heads" to covered side of bed near one long edge. Fasten a Tootsie Roll "body" below each head with icing.

3 Stretch the second Fruit Roll-Up into an even rectangle. Drape it over characters' bodies like a "blanket" (underneath "chins"), tucking it down slightly between characters with a spoon handle. Press blanket over edges of bed and wrap extra to back of candy bar to secure. If desired, cut stripes or polka dots from contrasting Fruit Roll-Ups and attach to blanket.

4 Draw a face on each almond with food markers. Let dry.

try this

Make a table and lamp from additional pieces of Kit Kat, Mike & Ikes and Dots candies to complete your bedroom set.

Sample uses red and blue Fruit Roll-Ups with polka dots cut from contrasting Roll-Ups. Try Tropical Tie-Dye Fruit Roll-Ups, too.

Wacky Waddlers

for each

You'll Need

Melted dark chocolate candy wafers

2 candy eyeballs

1 snack-size Mounds candy bar, unwrapped (.6 oz.)

1 white Necco Wafer

1 orange or yellow Tootsie Fruit Roll

1 small chocolate-covered mint patty

Waddle you do with these sweet tiny penguins? Eat them, of course!

To Make

1 With melted wafers, attach eyeballs to front side of Mounds bar, about ¼" from one rounded edge. At other rounded edge, attach Necco Wafer, edges even.

continued

2 Flatten Tootsie Fruit Roll to about ⅛″ thickness. With shears, cut a strip about ½″ wide. Cut strip into three small triangles to make one "beak" and two "feet." Mold beak triangle as desired. Make webbed feet from remaining two triangles by snipping partway through wide section twice on each one; separate the strips slightly.

3 Use melted wafers to attach beak below eyes. Place feet underneath candy bar, facing slightly outward, and fasten with melted wafers so penguin will stand up.

4 For "wings", cut two ⅜″ slices from outside edges of mint patty and trim top edge at an angle. Use melted wafers to attach one wing on each side of penguin body; let dry.

try this

Quarter the mint patties and attach one cut side to each side of penguin so pengin looks ready to fly.

flap flap

Kissing Wands

You'll Need

- 1 (2½″) Styrofoam ball
- 1 (6″) square aluminum foil
- Mounting tape
- 35 Hershey's Kisses in foil
- 1 (12″) wooden skewer (⅛″ in diameter)
- Glue
- Ribbon or bow

Wave the wand to see who YOUR Prince Charming will be

To Make

1 Wrap Styrofoam ball in aluminum foil, pressing down all around to smooth.

continued

2 Cut a strip from mounting tape about ½″ long to fit on flat side of a Kiss. Attach sticky side of tape to flat side of Kiss, remove paper from tape and attach Kiss to foil-covered ball. Continue with remaining Kisses, attaching each directly beside the previous Kiss, alternating colors until ball is covered.

3 Insert pointed end of skewer between Kisses and push at least halfway into ball. Remove skewer and insert a bit of glue in hole. Reinsert skewer and let dry.

4 Tie ribbon or bow around skewer just below decorated ball as desired.

Kissable Mice

Pull-n-Peel licorice

candy sprinkle

Hershey's Kiss

writing icing

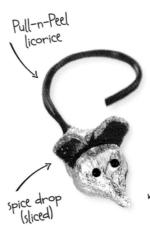

spice drop (sliced)

To make, cut two thin slices from a spice drop ("ears") and sandwich between flat sides of two Hershey's Kisses. Attach candy sprinkle "eyes" with writing icing. Insert 4″ string of licorice into wrapper at other pointed end ("tail").

Robotto Family

You'll Need

Shining examples of the future!

1 mini box Dots or Nerds

Heavy-duty aluminum foil

Clear tape

1 wooden skewer

2 sleeves Sixlets

Mounting tape

1 to 3 Hershey's Nuggets
(gold or silver wrapper)

2 Hershey's Kisses, optional

Melted white almond bark

2 candy eyeballs

optional gold paper, 1 Runts heart

To Make

1 For tall robot's "body," wrap Dots box in aluminum foil (or gold paper), making foil as flat as possible. Tape in place. (For short robot, wrap Nerds box the same way.) Use a skewer to carefully poke a hole near one end on both narrow sides of box to insert "arms."*

2 For tall robot's arms, wrap Sixlet sleeves in foil, leaving extra foil at each end. Press foil around each candy. Twist foil at one end of each arm; flatten foil at opposite end. Attach each arm to body by inserting twisted end into hole in box.* (For short robot, remove half the candies from each sleeve – these candies will not be used. Fold over extra wrapper on each and tape closed. Wrap in foil and attach as directed for tall robot.)

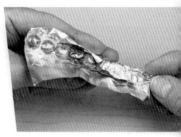

3 Use melted bark to attach candy eyeballs near top of rounded side of Hershey's Nugget "head." Use mounting tape to attach tiny pieces of rolled or crumpled foil for "hair," "ears," "mouth" and "nose." Fasten bottom of head to top of body with mounting tape and attach Runts heart, if desired.

4 For tall robot's "feet," use mounting tape to attach rounded side of remaining two Nuggets below body. (For short robot, attach Kisses for feet.)

Or omit holes in box and attach arms using mounting tape.

Wise Mr. Owl

You'll Need

- 1 snack-size Reese's Peanut Butter Cup (.55 oz.)
- Melted chocolate almond bark
- 2 white York Pieces
- 1 orange Tootsie Fruit Roll
- 1 Tootsie Roll Midgee
- 1 Junior Mint
- Black edible food marker

These wise owls are keeping an eye on you!

To Make

1 Remove wrapper from Peanut Butter Cup but leave brown liner on. With melted bark, attach white York Pieces near top edge of exposed Peanut Butter Cup for eyeballs.

2 Flatten Tootsie Fruit Roll to about ⅛″ thickness. With shears, cut a strip about ½″ wide; cut strip into three small triangles for a "beak" and two "feet." Cut two small snips partway through wide section of feet triangles to create "claws." With melted bark, attach beak below eyeballs and attach feet to lower edge of Peanut Butter Cup. Flatten Tootsie Roll and cut two triangular "ears." Fasten above eyeballs with melted bark.

3 Carefully slice Junior Mint in half crosswise to make two "wings"; gently press a wing in place on each side of beak, cut side down, with tip extending partway over edge of brown liner.

4 Use food marker to draw a closed "eyelid" or "pupil" on each eyeball as desired; let dry.

try this

Make your owls bigger by using regular size Reese's cups (.75 oz.).

Make a Splash

 DUCK

You'll Need

Life on the pond is just ducky!

1 yellow peanut M&M

1 (1˝) yellow gumball

1 melted yellow candy wafer

Spice drop candies (2 orange, 2 yellow)

Paste food coloring (black, blue)

White ready-to-use frosting

1 (3½˝ to 4˝) sugar cookie

To Make

1 Attach M&M "head" to gumball "body" with melted wafer; hold in place until set, about 1 minute.

2 Cut one orange and one yellow spice drop in half from top to bottom. Press cut side of orange pieces to bottom of gumball, narrow ends in front, to make duck's "feet." Press cut side of one yellow piece onto each side of gumball for "wings."

3 Cut remaining yellow spice drop into a small triangle and press on back of gumball for "tail." Cut remaining orange spice drop into a small "beak" shape; press in place on M&M.

4 Dip a toothpick into black food coloring and make dot "eyes" on M&M; let dry.

5 Tint frosting with blue food coloring. Spread frosting on all or part of cookie, creating waves as desired. Set duck (or other pond pals, below) on frosted cookie.

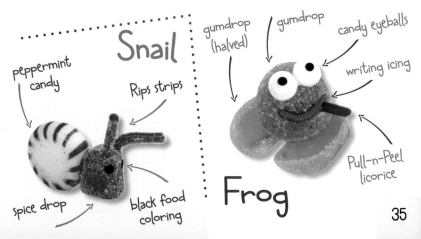

Snail

peppermint candy

Rips strips

spice drop

black food coloring

Frog

gumdrop (halved)

gumdrop

candy eyeballs

writing icing

Pull-n-Peel licorice

Gumdrops Ahoy!

for each

You'll Need

- 2 Life Savers, any color
- 1 gumdrop fruit slice, any color
- Writing icing to match gumdrop
- 1 pretzel stick
- Fruit Roll-Up, any color(s)
- 1 jelly bear or Teddy Graham

Ahoy, Mateys!

To Make

Carefully insert a pretzel "mast" into gumdrop until secure. Use shears to cut Fruit Roll-Up to fashion a "flag." Wrap flag around top of pretzel and press to fasten. Place bear on the boat and you're ready to float! (Attach bear with icing, if desired.)

Creepy Crawlers

You'll Need

Pull–n-Peel licorice, any color

16 Life Savers Gummies, any variety

Black edible food marker

One part creepy, many parts crawly.

To Make

Separate five strings from licorice. Use one string for base of "body." Cut remaining strings in half for "legs." Knot one end of long licorice string and thread on two Life Savers. Tie a short licorice string around long string next to Life Saver. Repeat with remaining pairs of Life Savers and legs. Tie one more short string in front of last Life Saver added ("head"). Use food marker to draw eyes on head. Clip front licorice pieces to desired length for "feelers."

Crazy Faces

You'll Need

Melted white almond bark

Assorted candies for decorating*

1 large sucker

These crazy face suckers can really take a licking!

To Make

1 Using melted bark, attach assorted candies to sucker to create CRAZY "faces."

continued

2 Additional features such as "hair," "ears" or "whiskers" can be added to give each a unique personality.

*Decorating Ideas

Sour Punch Straw piece for knot at top, Necco wafers and Skittles for "eyes," spice drop candy for "nose," mini jawbreakers for "cheeks" and a Gourmet Fruit Slice for "mouth."

Licorice pieces for "eyelashes," "mustache" and "beard"; Jordan almonds and M&Ms for "eyes," candy-covered almond for "nose" and a Runt for "mouth."

Runts for "eyebrows" and "nose," Life Savers and Skittles for "eyes," Gourmet Fruit Slices for "ears," Nerds for "freckles" and Rips and Peachy-O for "mouth."

try this

Put on a puppet show before eating them, one sweet feature at a time.

Ready to Race

for each

You'll Need

½ Kit Kat candy bar, unwrapped

Melted chocolate almond bark

1 Hershey's Nugget, unwrapped

1 Dove Promise, unwrapped

1 sour gummy worm

1 Life Saver, unwrapped

Black edible food marker

1 (¾") jawbreaker

3" striped sour candy strip

2 Junior Mints

4 (1½") foil-wrapped chocolate coins, unwrapped

2 Sour Strawz

1 white gumdrop

On your mark, get set, GO!

To Make

1 Gently scrape long sides of candy bar with a vegetable peeler to make smooth. Place Kit Kat flat side up and build "car" from back to front. Use melted bark to attach all candies. Attach one short side of nugget to one end of Kit Kat with flat side facing forward; hold until set.

2 To make "seat back," attach Promise in front of Nugget, flat side forward. Fasten gummy worm around top edge of Promise. Attach Life Saver "seat" in front of Promise. With food marker, draw a "helmet" and "face" on jawbreaker "head." Fasten head to Life Saver. Attach candy strip down length of car, from seat to front end.

. . . .

3 Fasten two chocolate coins together for each large "wheel"; let dry. With car on its side, attach one wheel to Kit Kat, centered and even with end; hold until set. Turn car over and attach second large wheel. Set car upright and attach one Junior Mint wheel on each side near front of car.

. . . .

4 To finish car, fasten a Strawz "bumper" to front of car and another Strawz on top of Nugget for a "spoiler." Cut a wedge from gumdrop to make a "windshield"; press in front of driver.

try this

Attach Sixlet candies to flat side of mini Kit Kat with melted chocolate bark to make a stoplight. Attach to mini Reese's Peanut Butter Cup so it will stand.

mini Kit Kat

Sixlet candies

mini Reese's Peanut Butter Cup

PURSEnality

You'll Need

- 1 or 2 Kit Kat candy bars (white or milk chocolate), unwrapped
- Melted white or chocolate almond bark
- White ready-to-use frosting, optional
- Paste food colorings, optional
- Assorted candies for decorating and handles*

Give your purse some personality!

To Make

1 For a thin "purse," decorate the flat side of one Kit Kat. For a thick purse, fasten two Kit Kats together with matching almond bark, edges even and flat sides facing out. Let dry. To decorate, use melted bark or frosting (white or tinted with food coloring) to attach candies as desired.

2 After decorating, attach candy handles of choice to purse with melted bark. (Flatten ends of thick handles as needed.)

*Decorating Ideas

Pink & green purse: a white Kit Kat with neon green and pink frosting. Flower "clasp" is five green Rips strips looped and pressed into frosting with a pink Necco Wafer and flower sprinkle on top. For "handle," soften a 6″ piece of pink Laffy Taffy in microwave for a few seconds; flatten and shape handle. Add pearl sprinkles as desired.

Red & white purse: two white Kit Kats, red Rips candy, red Pull-n-Peel licorice, red Jelly Bellies and red Sour Punch Straws.

White flowered purse: a white Kit Kat, red writing icing, Sprees, green Rips strips and Pull-n-Peel licorice.

Polka dot purse: a chocolate Kit Kat, tinted frosting, Sweet Tart, Necco Wafers and Extremes Rainbow Berry Sour Candy.

Brown flowered purse: two chocolate Kit Kats, flower-shaped and round candy sprinkles, Smarties and red Pull-n-Peel licorice. (Press licorice ends into holes on sides of purse and fasten with bark.)

Orange & green purse: a white Kit Kat, green writing icing, Sixlets, orange Spree and Airhead.

Tangle of Bangles

You'll Need

- 5 to 7 yds. paper curling ribbon
- 12″ to 18″ (1½″ wide) fabric ribbon
- 8 to 10 Milk Maids (or other colorful wrapped candies)
- 3 rolls Spree candies

Fun to wear, good enough to eat!

To Make

1 Cut 15 to 20 (12″) pieces of curling ribbon.

44

continued

2

Tie one end of a Milk Maid to center of wide fabric ribbon with a piece of curling ribbon; pull knot snugly. Repeat to attach remaining Milk Maids and ribbons on both sides of center candy, alternating their direction. Slide knots and candies together along wide ribbon to fit wrist.

3

Use curling ribbon to tie one end of each Spree roll onto wide ribbon, positioning as desired. Tie on additional pieces of curling ribbon between candies. Curl ribbon with edge of scissors. Tie around wrist to wear.

Ring

Life Saver

Tootsie Pop Drop

Pull-n-Peel licorice

melted candy wafer

Snaps Bracelet

Snaps candies

candy necklace pieces

Pull-n-Peel licorice

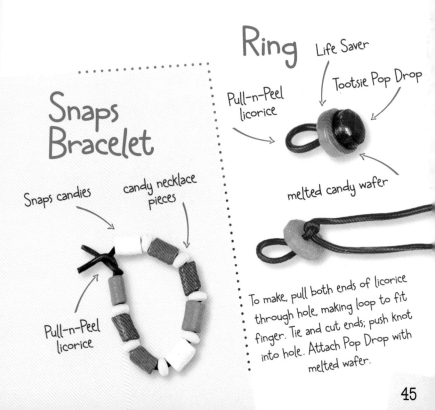

To make, pull both ends of licorice through hole, making loop to fit finger. Tie and cut ends; push knot into hole. Attach Pop Drop with melted wafer.

45

Candy Campfire

for each

You'll Need

2 (3″) Tootsie Rolls

3 pieces of candy corn

3 T. white decorator icing, divided

Paste food coloring (orange, golden yellow)

2 small plastic bags

1 York Peppermint Patty

Chocolate candy rocks

An indoor campfire? Sweet!

To Make

1 With shears, cut both Tootsie Rolls into 2″ lengths and then cut 2″ pieces in half lengthwise to make four "logs." Cut remaining 1″ pieces into many thin strips for "tinder."

2 With food coloring, tint about 1 tablespoon icing orange and place in a plastic bag; set aside. Tint remaining icing golden yellow. Spread a large circle of yellow icing on the center of Peppermint Patty. Build "fire" by setting candy corn upright in center of yellow icing; add tinder pieces around and over candy corn as desired. Arrange four logs upright in a teepee shape over tinder, with log ends set in icing.

3 Put remaining yellow icing in remaining plastic bag. Cut a small corner off both plastic bags and pipe on yellow and orange icing "flames" as desired.

4 Place a ring of candy rocks around outer edge of yellow icing for "fire ring," piping on more icing as needed to secure rocks.

try this

Cut and shape a long thin "stick" from a 3" Tootsie Roll. Slide mini marshmallows on one end to "roast" over your campfire. Sing a few campfire songs, too!

Candy Express

for each

You'll Need

Get on board the
Candy Express!

Double-stick tape

5-stick packs of gum

Assorted wrapped candies*

Pull-n-Peel licorice, optional

Tootsie Roll Midgees, optional

optional
Attach train cars together with Tootsie
Roll Midgees, if desired. Or make a
track out of Pull-n-Peel licorice. Use
your imagination!

To Make

1 With tape, attach two packs of gum together for each "train car."

2 Use tape to attach all remaining candies to complete cars. Attach "wheels" so that about half the round candy is lower than the bottom of the car. (Tape will hold most candies together; however, have a hot glue gun or glue dots on hand in case tape doesn't stick to some wrappers.)

*Decorating Ideas

"Engine": one 5-stick pack of gum, one roll of mints or Life Savers, one Hershey's Kiss, two Dove Promises and four (1″) foil-wrapped chocolate coins.

Yellow "car": two 5-stick packs of gum, three Rolos and four butterscotch disks.

Green "car": two 5-stick packs of gum, three rolls of Smarties and four Life Savers.

Blue "car": two 5-stick packs of gum, three coal-shaped candies and four Life Savers.

"Caboose": two 5-stick packs of red gum or two snack-size Kit Kats (.49 oz.), four Andes chocolates (red wrapper), one Starburst and four cinnamon disks.

Haunted Forest

You'll Need

- 1½ chocolate-flavored licorice twists
- Melted chocolate almond bark
- 1 chocolate graham cracker square
- Fall-colored candy decorating sprinkles
- 1 candy pumpkin

These are some scary treeeeeats!

To Make

1 Use shears to cut whole licorice twist in half crosswise. From one end of each licorice "tree," cut a slit about 1½″ long between each "ridge" and fan out cut ends for "branches"; set aside.

50

2 Let melted bark set until nearly cool but not hardened. Frost cracker with a thick layer of bark. Immediately scatter decorating sprinkle "leaves" around outer edges of frosted cracker, leaving center clear for trees. Attach pumpkin near one edge.

. . . .

3 Promptly attach trees to center of cracker, holding in place until secure and trees stand on their own.

try this

To make the forest come alive, use a black edible food marker to draw a ghost face on white Jordan almonds. Attach "ghosts" in or around trees.

Candyland Corn

You'll Need

Yummier than the real thing!

White ready-to-use frosting

Paste food coloring
(yellow or orange)

1 fun-size candy bar
such as Snickers

15 to 20 mini M&Ms (yellow,
orange, red, green, brown)

1 Blazin' Blue/Green Fruit Roll-Up

To Make

1 Tint frosting with yellow or orange food coloring for "corn cob." Put a thick layer of frosting on top of candy bar. Starting about ¾" from one end of candy bar, make three lengthwise rows of random-colored M&M "corn kernels," placing candies close together on edge in frosting and making middle row slightly longer than the other two rows.

2 Cut apart green and blue sides of Fruit Roll-Up. Wrap a strip of blue around all four sides of candy bar, avoiding back side.

3 Cut various lengths of narrow triangles from green side of Fruit Roll-Up for "corn husks." Attach longer triangles over blue layer first, adding shorter triangles over the top as desired, covering all frosting. Add a couple of short husks above corn at top. Curl husk tips as desired.

try this

To make an ear of sweet corn, use all yellow M&Ms and attach as directed above.

Turkey Trot

You'll Need

Gobble them up, one sweet feather at a time!

- Waxed paper
- 5 gummy fish
- Melted chocolate almond bark
- 100 Grand candy bar
- Thin wooden skewers, optional
- Writing icing (white, red, yellow)
- 1 yellow candy-coated sunflower seed or mini M&M
- Jelly Bellies (1 red, 1 brown)
- Black writing gel
- 2 yellow flower-shaped candy decorating sprinkles

54

To Make

1 Place waxed paper on work surface. To attach "feathers" to turkey "body," use shears to cut off ⅜" from tail of one fish candy for center top feather. Dip about ½" of each fish tail into melted bark and set on waxed paper in a fanned-out position with tail ends touching. Set flat side of candy bar on coated tails, arranging fish to look like feathers; press gently and hold in place until set, about 1 minute.

2 If using skewers, insert pointed end in bottom of candy bar and gently press partway through candy.

3 Place two small dots of white icing on "head" section of body, about ½" from top of candy bar. Add a tiny spot of black gel to finish each "eye." Let dry.

4 With shears, cut Jelly Bellies in half lengthwise. For "wattle," use red icing to fasten cut side of one red Jelly Belly piece to body below eyes, about halfway down candy bar. With yellow icing, attach sunflower seed "beak" just above wattle, propping up tip on wattle; let dry.

5 With yellow icing, attach two yellow flower sprinkles for "feet" near bottom of body.

6 Using melted bark, attach cut side of one brown Jelly Belly piece on each side of body for "wings." Let dry.

Moose on the Loose

The moose are loose!
The moose are loose!

You'll Need

2 fun-size Twix candy bars, unwrapped

Melted chocolate almond bark

1 (3″) Tootsie Roll, unwrapped

Thin pretzels (3 twists, 4 sticks)

1 snack-size Tootsie Roll, unwrapped (.5 oz.)

2 marshmallow circus peanuts

2 candy eyeballs

1 brown mini M&M

1 red candy decorating sprinkle or red writing icing

To Make

1 Fasten flat sides of Twix bars together with melted bark for "body"; wipe off excess bark and let dry. Carefully break pretzel twists to make two matching "antlers" and a "tail"; set aside.

2 Cut ends off 3″ Tootsie Roll and cut remainder into four (½″) pieces. With a pretzel stick, poke a deep starter hole in one cut end of each piece to hold legs later; remove pretzel. With melted bark, attach pieces to bottom of body (holes up) where legs will be; let dry.

3 Cut 1¼″ length from snack-size Tootsie Roll for "head"; reshape slightly with hands. With a pretzel stick, make two starter holes on top of head for the antlers. Shape remaining ³⁄₈″ of Tootsie Roll into a "neck." Turn body over to rest on Tootsie Roll pieces. Attach neck and head on top of body with melted bark.

4 Use melted bark to attach edge of eyeballs to top of head; hold until set. Attach M&M "nose" and red sprinkle "mouth"; let dry.

5 Cut circus peanuts in half crosswise for "hooves." Push a pretzel stick "leg" partway into rounded side of each hoof. Holding moose upside down, dip other end of legs into melted bark and insert in starter holes; hold legs straight until set. Stand moose up, adjusting hooves for good balance.

Cozy Cottages

![winter cottage scene photograph]

You'll Need

Easy to build, fun to decorate, yummy to eat.

7 (1½˝ square) shortbread cookies

Melted white almond bark

Assorted candies: candy corn, Life Savers, Dove Promises, candy decorating sprinkles, Kit Kats, peppermint sticks

To Make

1 Lay one cookie on work surface, flat side up. Dip one edge of a second cookie in melted bark and attach upright, flat side in, on top and along edge of first cookie. Hold until set. Repeat with a third cookie across from second cookie. Hold until set.

2 Coat top edges of the two upright cookies in melted bark and set flat side of a fourth cookie against wet bark, creating an open-ended box. Let dry. Turn box so an open end faces up. Attach flat side of a fifth cookie to open end of box. Let dry.

3 For "roof," dip two opposite edges of sixth and seventh cookies in melted bark, coating heavily. Set one coated edge of each cookie on top of opposite sides of box, bringing upper edges together to form a point. Add extra melted bark to roofline to fill in space. Let dry. Use melted bark to attach assorted candies to decorate cottages.

try this

To make a snow-covered tree, insert a green sucker into a gumdrop and drizzle sucker with melted bark; scatter colored sprinkles on wet bark and let dry.

Gummy Pines

for each

You'll Need

Melted white almond bark

2 Fudge Stripe cookies*

Waxed paper

1 (½ x 4″) peppermint stick

14 (¾ x 3″) sticks of gum,** unwrapped

1 Cherry Sour Ball

Candy decorating sprinkles

You could "get stuck" in this tree!

To Make

1 Use melted almond bark to attach cookies together, one on top of the other, flat sides down; let dry on waxed paper. Dip bottom ½″ of peppermint stick in bark and insert coated end through holes of cookies so peppermint stick sets upright; set aside.

2 On a cutting board, lay 10 sticks of gum side by side, long edges touching. Use a pizza cutter to cut 1″ from length of all sticks; reserve 1″ pieces. Cut 2″ pieces in half diagonally. Dip ¼″ of the short end of one diagonal "branch" in melted bark. Press coated end against peppermint "trunk" about ½″ above cookie (points  will drape over sides of cookies); hold in place a few seconds. Work around trunk with four more branches, all facing the same direction and overlapping previous branch to complete the bottom row. Make two more rows about ½″ apart, with the pointed tips between branches in previous row.

3 Cut three full sticks of gum in half diagonally and attach five pieces in a row ½″ above previous row as in Step 2. Follow with a row of 2″ branches.

4 Cut five of reserved 1″ pieces in half diagonally and attach to trunk in two more rows, with final row beginning on the top edge of peppermint and draping over its edge. (There will be some gum pieces remaining.)

5 Carefully flare out tips of branches slightly. Drizzle melted bark along branches for "snow" and attach decorating sprinkles as desired. Cover top of peppermint stick with melted bark and attach Sour Ball.

Or other cookie with a hole approximately ½″ in diameter.
** Gum must be soft and pliable.

Rich Rudolph

for each

You'll Need

2 (1½˝) foil-wrapped
chocolate coins

Writing icing (white, red)

Mini M&Ms (brown, red)

Chocolate decorating
sprinkles, optional

Red Pull-n-Peel licorice,
optional

1 mini Tootsie Roll or caramel
cube, unwrapped

Green Fruit Roll-Up, optional

*Let the reindeer
games begin!*

To Make

1 Remove foil cover from one side of one coin for Rudolph's
"face." To make "eyes," put two drops of white icing on face
and press a brown mini M&M or chocolate sprinkle into
each drop.*

2 With red icing, fasten a red mini M&M below eyes for Rudolph's "nose."

- -

3 Draw a red icing "mouth" below nose or attach a short piece of licorice with red icing. Set aside to dry.

- -

4 Soften Tootsie Roll or caramel in microwave for a few seconds. Let cool just enough to handle. Tear off a small piece, flatten slightly and set aside to use as a spacer. Divide remaining candy in half. Knead and shape each half into one "antler," about the same thickness as spacer. With icing, attach bottom of antlers to top part of wrapped coin (antlers extend above coin). Fasten spacer on wrapped coin, below antlers.

- -

5 With more icing, attach Rudolph's face to wrapped coin, lining up edges and pressing gently to hold. Let dry.

try this
Shape a small piece of green Fruit Roll-Up into a leaf shape and add a red icing or mini M&M "berry."

* Or purchase candy eyeballs and attach to Rudolph's face with white icing.

Index

Candied Cooties..6

Candy Campfire...46

Candy Express...48

Candyland Corn...52

Coral Critters..23

Cozy Cottages...58

Crazy Faces..38

Creepy Crawlers..37

Eye Candy..16

Gumdrops Ahoy!...36

Gummy Pines...60

Haunted Forest...50

Kissable Mice...29

Kissing Wands..28

Li'l Licorice Baskets.....................................12

Make a Splash..34

Moose on the Loose.....................................56

Peep Mobiles..14

PURSEnality...42

Push Pop Planes..4

Ready to Race...40

Rich Rudolph..62

Robotto Family...30

Sweet Dreams..24

Sweet Rides...20

Tangle of Bangles..44

The Write Candy...18

Turkey Trot..54

Wacky Waddlers...26

Watch This!...8

Wise Mr. Owl...32

Zany Zebras...10